A Desert ABC

An Alphabet Book

by B. A. Hoena

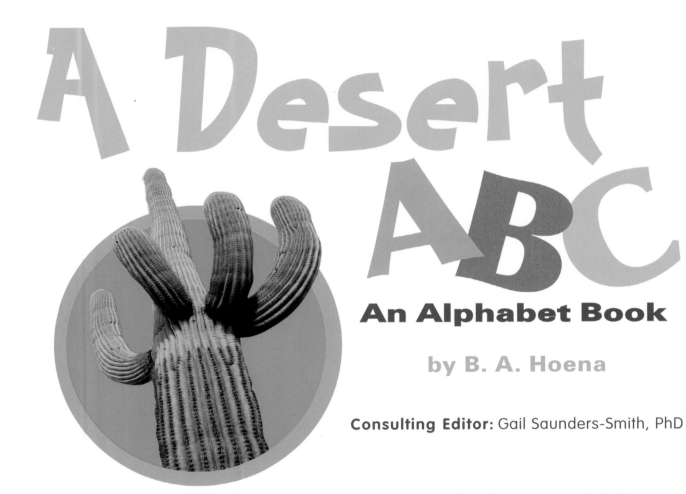

Consulting Editor: Gail Saunders-Smith, PhD

Capstone
press

Mankato, Minnesota

A is for armadillo.

Armadillos are like little tanks.
Bony armor covers their backs
and keeps them safe.

B is for butte.

Buttes are beautiful works of art.
Wind and rain carved these rocky hills
over millions of years.

C is for camel.

Camels don't need backpacks.
They carry food and water as fat
in the humps on their backs.

4

D is for dune.

Dunes are waves of sand that move slowly across the desert. Winds blow them forward a few feet each year.

E is for elf owl.

"Chee, chee, chee," elf owls whistle. These tiny owls nest in cactus and desert trees.

F is for fox.

Bushy-tailed foxes run through the hot desert. They try to spot their next meals hiding among rocks.

G is for gecko.

Geckos don't like the hot desert sun.
They hide in the shade during the day.

H is for hand-standing beetle.

A hand-standing beetle knows a trick. As it stands on its head, dew collects on its body and rolls down to its mouth.

I is for iguana.

A desert iguana thinks it's safe lying around. Its skin is the same color as the ground.

J is for jackrabbit.

A jackrabbit doesn't use its big ears just to hear. Heat escapes through its ears and keeps this rabbit cool.

K is for kangaroo rat.

Kangaroo rats hop about, stuffing their faces with seeds. They carry food around in their cheeks.

L is for living stone.

Living stones look like rocks, but they're not. They're cactus with brightly colored flowers.

M is for mongoose.

Snakes aren't safe when a mongoose is on the loose. A mongoose is quick to bite snakes before they strike.

N is for nomad.

Nomads don't stay in just one home.
They roam the desert searching for food
and water.

O is for oasis.

An oasis forms an island of green
in a dry, dusty desert. It has water
for plants to grow and animals to drink.

P is for prickly pear.

Prickly pears aren't prickly fruit.
They're cactus covered with
sharp, pointy needles.

Q is for quail.

Quails are quick on their feet as they run through the desert. When afraid, quails are quick to fly away.

R is for rattlesnake.

Rattlesnakes don't play with rattles.
They shake their tails as if to say,
"Stay away. I'll bite!"

S is for scorpion.

A scorpion pinches with its pinchers. It stings with the stinger at the end of its curly tail.

T is for tumbleweed.

Dried-up tumbleweeds go wherever the wind blows. They roll across the desert, dropping seeds as they go.

21

U is for underneath.

Some desert snakes are sneaky.
They hide underneath the sand,
waiting for a meal to walk by.

V is for vulture.

Bald-headed vultures circle high overhead.
They eat animals that are already dead.

W is for welwitschia.

Do you think **"Wel-WIT-chee-uh"** is difficult to say? These odd-sounding plants spread their leaves across the ground to collect water from dew and fog.

X is for Mexican poppy.

Be careful when picking Mexican poppies. Their prickly stems might stick you. **OUCH!**

Y is for yucca.

A yucca's pointy leaves have a purpose. They catch raindrops, and the water follows the leaves down to the yucca's roots.

Z is for lizard.

Shovel-snouted lizards know how to dance. They lift their feet off the hot, hot sand to keep them cool.

Fun Facts about Deserts

Desert plants have a difficult time finding water. Most plants get water through their roots. Some desert plants have root systems that grow more than 100 feet (30 meters) deep.

Cactus don't have leaves. They have sharp spines to keep animals from eating them.

Deserts receive less than 10 inches (25 centimeters) of precipitation each year. Desert precipitation comes in the form of rain, fog, and snow.

Scientists think that some desert plants give off a chemical that keeps other plants from growing too close to them. In this way, each plant has enough room to grow and find water.

At about 5.4 million square miles (14 million square kilometers), the continent of Antarctica is the world's largest desert. It is covered in ice, but like other deserts, it receives very little precipitation each year.

A new "rattle" is added to a rattlesnake's tail each time it sheds its skin.

A camel has three eyelids. The eyelids protect a camel's eyes from sun and blowing sand.

Glossary

armor (AR-mur)—a protective covering; small plates of bone make up an armadillo's armor.

dew (DOO)—small water drops that collect overnight on outside surfaces, such as plant leaves

nomad (NOH-mad)—a person who moves from place to place instead of living in one spot

oasis (oh-AY-siss)—a place in a desert where there is water for plants, animals, and people

pincher (PINCH-ur)—a part of an animal, such as a claw, that it uses to hold and pinch

stinger (STING-ur)—a sharp, pointy part of an animal that can be used to sting

Read More

Bailey, Jill. *Life in a Desert Cactus.* Microhabitats. Chicago: Raintree, 2004.

Galko, Francine. *Desert Animals.* Animals in Their Habitats. Chicago: Heinemann, 2003.

Whitehouse, Patricia. *Hiding in a Desert.* Animal Camouflage. Chicago: Heinemann, 2003.

Internet Sites

FactHound offers a safe, fun way to find Internet sites related to this book. All of the sites on FactHound have been researched by our staff.

Here's how:
1. Visit *www.facthound.com*
2. Type in this special code **073682605X** for age-appropriate sites. Or enter a search word related to this book for a more general search.
3. Click on the **Fetch It** button.

FactHound will fetch the best sites for you!

Index

A+ Books are published by Capstone Press
P.O. Box 669, 151 Good Counsel Drive, Mankato, Minnesota 56002
www.capstonepress.com

1 2 3 4 5 6 09 08 07 06 05

Library of Congress Cataloging-in-Publication Data
Hoena, B. A.
    A desert ABC: an alphabet book / by B.A. Hoena.
    p. cm.— (A+ alphabet books)
    Includes bibliographical references (p. 31) and index.
    ISBN 0-7368-2605-X (hardcover)
    1. Deserts—Juvenile literature. 2. English language—Alphabet—Juvenile literature.
[1. Deserts. 2. Alphabet.] I. Title. II. Series: Alphabet (Mankato, Minn.).
QH88.H54 2004
578.754—dc22   2003027800

Summary: Introduces deserts through photographs and brief text that uses one word relating to deserts for each letter of the alphabet.

Credits
Amanda Doering and June Preszler, editors; Heather Kindseth, designer; Kelly Garvin, photo researcher; Eric Kudalis, product planning editor

Photo Credits
Bruce Coleman Inc./JC Carton, 15, 16; Bruce Coleman Inc./John Giustina, 8; Bruce Coleman Inc./John Shaw, 5; Bruce Coleman Inc./Karen McGougan, 7; Bruce Coleman Inc./Michael P. Fogden, 24; Bruce Coleman Inc./Peter Ward, 21; Bruce Coleman Inc./Winland Rice, 17; Corbis/David Samuel Robbins, cover (camel); Corbis/Frank Lane Picture Agency/Ron Austing, 6; Corbis/Gallo Images, 23; Corbis/Lanz Von Horsten; Gallo Images, 20; Corbis/Lynda Richardson, 14; Corbis/Martin Harvey; Gallo Images, 27; Corbis/RF, cover (dunes); Corbis/Scott T. Smith, 3; Corbis/Shai Ginott, 22; DigitalVision/NatPhotos and Tony Sweet, 28 (left); McDonald Wildlife Photography/Joe McDonald, 10, 12, 25; Minden Pictures/Globio/Gerry Ellis, 26; Minden Pictures/Norbert Wu, 4; Minden Pictures/Tom Vezo, 18; Natural Visions/Heather Angel, 13; PhotoDisc Inc., 1, 28 (right) 29; Robert & Linda Mitchell, 9; Robert McCaw, 19; Tom Stack & Associates, Inc./Jeff Foot, 2; Tom Stack & Associates, Inc./John Gerlach, 11

Note to Parents, Teachers, and Librarians
A Desert ABC: An Alphabet Book uses colorful photographs and a nonfiction format to introduce children to characteristics about deserts while building a mastery of the alphabet. This book is designed to be read independently by an early reader or to be read aloud to a pre-reader. The images help early readers and listeners understand the text and concepts discussed. The book encourages further learning by including the following sections: Fun Fact about Deserts, Glossary, Read More, Internet Sites, and Index. Early readers may need assistance using these features.

For Addison, my sweet little chickadee, and her daddy, Jonathan,

and thanks to Bill and Susan Garrison for their Red Dog Dan inspiration

—*J. M. H.*

To my favorite prairie chicken, Joan, with love, Hen

—*H. C.*

Published by
PEACHTREE PUBLISHERS
1700 Chattahoochee Avenue
Atlanta, Georgia 30318-2112

www.peachtree-online.com

Text © 2013 by Jackie Mims Hopkins
Illustrations © 2013 by Henry Cole

Design and composition by Loraine M. Joyner

The illustrations were created in watercolor, ink, and colored pencil on 100% rag,
archival watercolor paper. Title typeset in Adobe System Inc.'s Nueva by Carol
Twombly; text typeset in Microsoft Corporation's Tahoma by Matthew Carter.

Printed in December 2012 by Imago in Singapore
10 9 8 7 6 5 4 3 2 1
First Edition

ISBN 978-1-56145-694-9 / 1-56145-694-2

Library of Congress Cataloging-in-Publication Data

Hopkins, Jackie.
  Prairie chicken little / written by Jackie Mims Hopkins; illustrated by Henry Cole.
     p. cm.
  Summary: In this retelling of the classic tale, Mary McBlicken, a small prairie
chicken, and her animal friends are on their way to tell Cowboy Stan and Red
Dog Dan that a stampede is coming when they meet a hungry coyote.
  [1. Folklore.] I. Cole, Henry, 1955- ill. II. Chicken Licken. III. Title.
  PZ8.1.H854Pr 2013
  398.2—dc23
  [E]
                          2012025540

Prairie Chicken Little

Jackie Mims Hopkins

Illustrated by **Henry Cole**

PEACHTREE
ATLANTA

Out on the grasslands where bison roam, Mary McBlicken the prairie chicken was scritch-scratching for her breakfast, when all of a sudden she heard a rumbling and a grumbling and a tumbling.

"Oh no!" she exclaimed. "A stampede's a comin'! I need to hightail it back to the ranch to tell Cowboy Stan and Red Dog Dan. They'll know what to do."

So away Mary ran, lickety-splickety, as fast as her little prairie chicken legs could carry her.

On her way to the ranch, Mary came upon Jeffrey Snog the prairie dog, who was soaking up some sunshine.

"Good mornin' to you," barked Jeffrey.

"No time for good mornin's," warned Mary.
"A stampede's a comin'!"

"How do you know that this is so?" asked Jeffrey.

"I heard a rumblin' and a grumblin' and
a tumblin'—I did!" said Mary.

"A stampede, yes indeed," said Jeffrey.

"Come with me to tell Cowboy Stan and
Red Dog Dan!" hollered Mary.

"Let's hit the trail!" barked Jeffrey. And away the pair ran, lickety-splickety, toward the ranch.

Soon they met Beau Grabbit the jack rabbit,
who was nibbling on some sweet grass.

"Where are you two going in such a hurry?"
he asked.

"A stampede's a comin'!" said Mary. "We're headin' to the ranch to tell Cowboy Stan and Red Dog Dan."

"How do you know that this is so?" asked Beau.

"I heard a rumblin' and a grumblin' and a tumblin'—I did!" said Mary.

"A stampede, yes indeed," said Beau.

"Come with us to tell Cowboy Stan
and Red Dog Dan!" hollered Mary.

"Let's hop to it then," said Beau.

And they lit off across the prairie, lickety-splickety, toward the ranch.

Before long, the trio came across
June Spark the meadowlark, who was
building her nest in the tall prairie grass.

"What's going on?" asked June.

"A stampede's a comin'!" chorused the trio.

"How do you know that this is so?" asked June.

"I heard a rumblin' and a grumblin'
and a tumblin'—I did!" said Mary.

"A stampede, yes indeed,"
said June.

"Come with us to tell Cowboy Stan and Red Dog Dan!" hollered Mary.

"What are we waitin' for?" chirped June.

And away they all flew, lickety-splickety, toward the ranch.

It wasn't long before Slim Brody the sly coyote spotted them making their way across the prairie.

"Well, hello there, my fine feathered and furry friends. What's the big rush?"

"A stampede's a comin'! We're headin' to the ranch to tell Cowboy Stan and Red Dog Dan," said Mary.

"It's your lucky day," said Slim.

"I just happen to know a shortcut."

He had no intention of taking them to the ranch.

Instead, he led them across the plain,

over a hill,

through a pass,

around a bend,

and down a gully

to the entrance of his den.

"What's this?"

squawked Mary.

"This," snarled Slim, "is the passage to the shortcut." He flashed a toothy smile and closed in on Mary McBlicken and the others.

The fine feathered and furry friends all started clucking and barking and thumping and chirping as loud as they could.

Cowboy Stan and Red Dog Dan heard the ruckus and came charging across the prairie toward the den. Dan made a beeline for Slim Brody and chased that coyote, lickety-splickety, far, far, away.

"What's going on?" asked Stan.

"A stampede's a comin'!" cried Mary.

"How do you know that this is so?" asked Stan.

But before Mary could open her beak to speak, everyone heard a rumbling and a grumbling and a tumbling—yes indeed!

"Why, that's not a stampede," said Stan, "that's your stomach! There's only one way to head off a rumbling and a grumbling and a tumbling stomach.

"You need some grub!"

So, Cowboy Stan cooked up a fine supper for those critters and that took care of Mary McBlicken's stomach stampede, lickety-splickety, yes indeed.

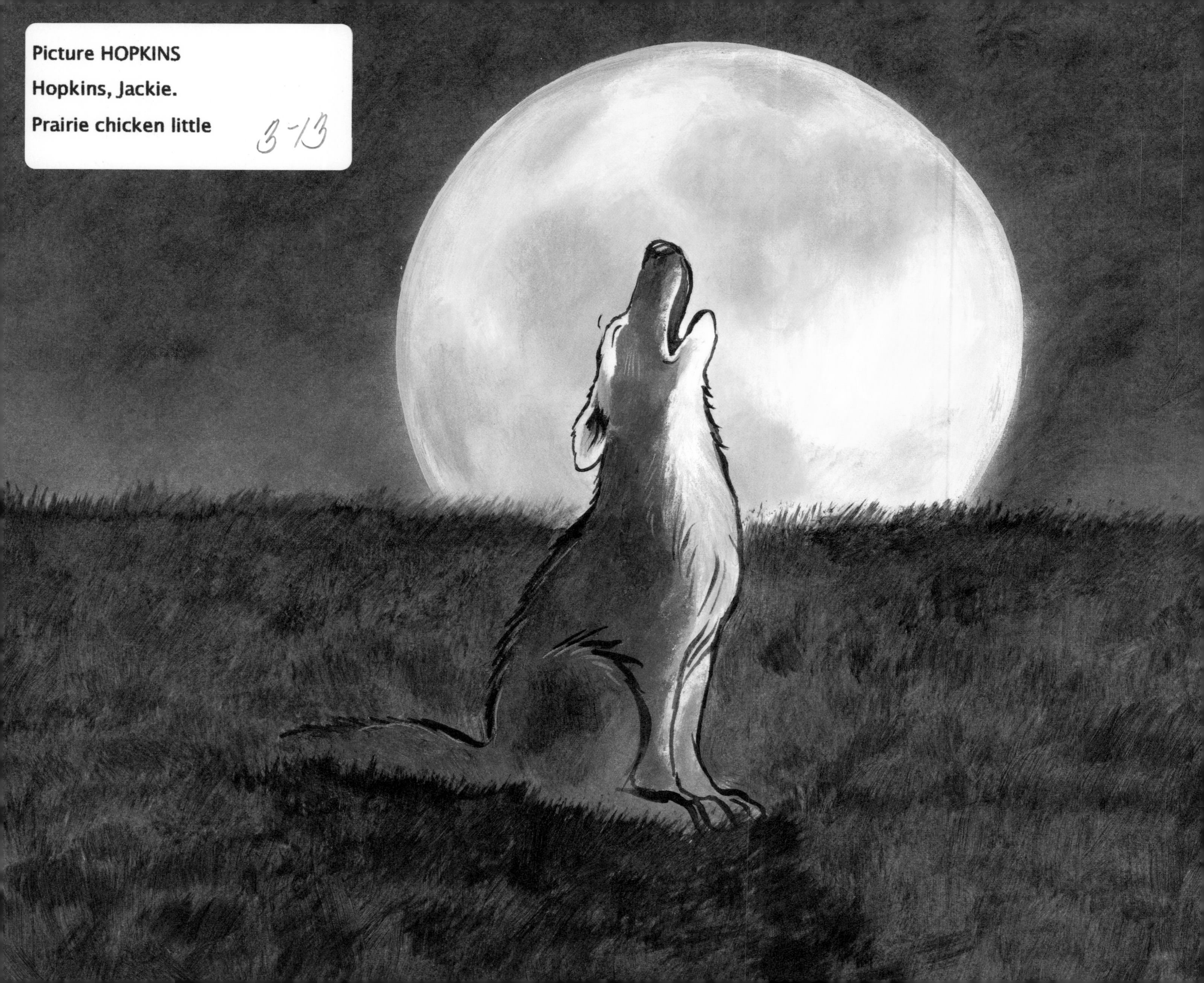